Take Our Cat, Please!

Other Get Fuzzy Books

The Dog Is Not a Toy (House Rule #4)

Fuzzy Logic: Get Fuzzy 2

The Get Fuzzy Experience: Are You Bucksperienced

I Would Have Bought You a Cat, But . . .

Blueprint for Disaster

Say Cheesy

Scrum Bums

I'm Ready for My Movie Contract

Treasuries

Groovitude: A Get Fuzzy Treasury

Bucky Katt's Big Book of Fun

Loserpalooza

Take Our Cat, Please!

A GET FUZZY Collection

by Darby Conley

Andrews McMeel
Publishing, LLC
Kansas City

Get Fuzzy is distributed internationally by United Feature Syndicate, Inc.

Take Our Cat, Please! copyright © 2008 by Darby Conley. All rights reserved. Printed in the United States of America. No part of this book may be used or reproduced in any manner whatsoever without written permission except in the case of reprints in the context of reviews. For information, write Andrews McMeel Publishing, LLC, an Andrews McMeel Universal company, 4520 Main Street, Kansas City, Missouri 64111.

08 09 10 11 12 BBG 10 9 8 7 6 5 4 3 2 1

ISBN-13: 978-0-7407-7095-1
ISBN-10: 0-7407-7095-0

Library of Congress Control Number: 2007937792
www.andrewsmcmeel.com

Get Fuzzy can be viewed on the Internet at
www.comics.com/comics/getfuzzy.

——————— **ATTENTION: SCHOOLS AND BUSINESSES** ———————

Andrews McMeel books are available at quantity discounts with bulk purchase for educational, business, or sales promotional use. For information, please write to: Special Sales Department, Andrews McMeel Publishing, LLC, 4520 Main Street, Kansas City, Missouri 64111.

8

SATCHEL TELLS ME YOU AND THE FERRET ARE AT IT AGAIN.

IT'S ON, BABY. IT'S ON LIKE A BAPTIST'S V-CHIP.

SO WHAT IS IT NOW? I THOUGHT YOU GUYS WERE CHILL.

CHILL? IS IT "CHILL" WHEN YOU WALK BY SOMEONE'S DOORWAY AND THEY **WATCH** YOU WALKING? IS THAT "CHILL"? I SAY IT IS **NOT**.

LET ME GET THIS STRAIGHT... YOU'RE MAD NOW BECAUSE HE... *LOOKED* AT YOU?

WHERE... WHERE AM I? I MUST BE GOING NUTS.

YUP. IT'S ON.

OOO! THE MAIL SLOT!

MAIL? AT THIS HOUR?

WHAT IS... COULD THAT BE... THAT LOOKS LIKE...

FERRET DROPPINGS!

OH, SNAP! YOU GOT SERVED!

I'LL BE IN THE KITCHEN EATING A CAN OF RAISINS.

DUDE. RAISINS GIVE YOU... ...OH.

HA HA! EWWW!

WHERE DID I GO WRONG, SATCH?

TWO COLLEGE DEGREES... A POSITION OF SOME RESPONSIBILITY AT WORK. AND HERE I AM ON MY HANDS AND KNEES CLEANING UP ANIMAL WASTE FOR THE THIRD TIME IN TWO DAYS...

I KEEP EXPECTING THAT ASHTON KUTCHER DUDE TO JUMP OUT FROM BEHIND SOMETHING AND YELL "YOU GOT PUNKED!"

I THINK YOU HAVE TO BE PRETTY COOL TO BE PUNK'D... I THINK WHEN STUFF HAPPENS TO A "ROB WILCO," IT'S JUST, UM...

WEDNESDAY.

16

17

19

24

27

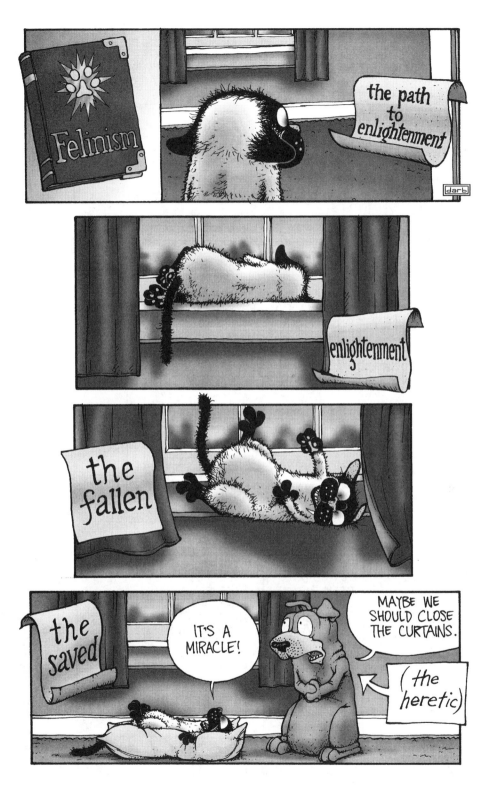

WHERE ARE YOU GOING? TO GET ME MORE BIRTHDAY PRESENTS, I ASSUME?

I ALREADY GOT YOU YOUR PRESENT, DUDE.

PRESENT-*TUH*? SINGULAR? AS IN *ONE PRESENT*? IT'S MY BIRTHDAY! DO YOU REALIZE HOW OBNOXIOUS THAT IS?

I HAVE A FAIRLY GOOD FRAME OF REFERENCE FOR "OBNOXIOUS," YES.

CRACKER, IT BETTER BE **HUGE**, YO.

I THOUGHT OF SOMETHING ELSE WE COULD GET BUCKY... WHAT'S THE ONE THING HE NEEDS MOST?

MEDICATION?

A **GIRLFRIEND**! I HEARD THAT LOTS OF PEOPLE MEET THROUGH THE NEWSPAPER, SO I LOOKED AND SURE ENOUGH, THERE'S A DATING SERVICE THAT CATERS TO SIAMESE CATS!

...A BREEDER IS WHERE KITTENS COME FROM, SATCHEL. IT'S NOT A CAT DATING SERVICE.

OHH... $600 DOES SEEM A LITTLE EXPENSIVE FOR A DATE!

IT'S SWEET OF YOU TO WANT TO SET BUCKY UP ON A DATE, SATCH, BUT I DON'T KNOW IF IT'S SUCH A GOOD IDEA... HE DOESN'T REALLY HAVE THE HEALTHIEST OUTLOOK TOWARDS WOMEN...

HE DOESN'T?

...I GUESS IT'S NOT *SPECIFIC* TO FEMALES... HE'S GOT A BAD ATTITUDE TOWARDS PRETTY MUCH EVERYTHING...

FOR EXAMPLE, I WOULDN'T SET HIM UP WITH A RUG, EITHER. OR A LAMP.

HMM.

31

33

48

56

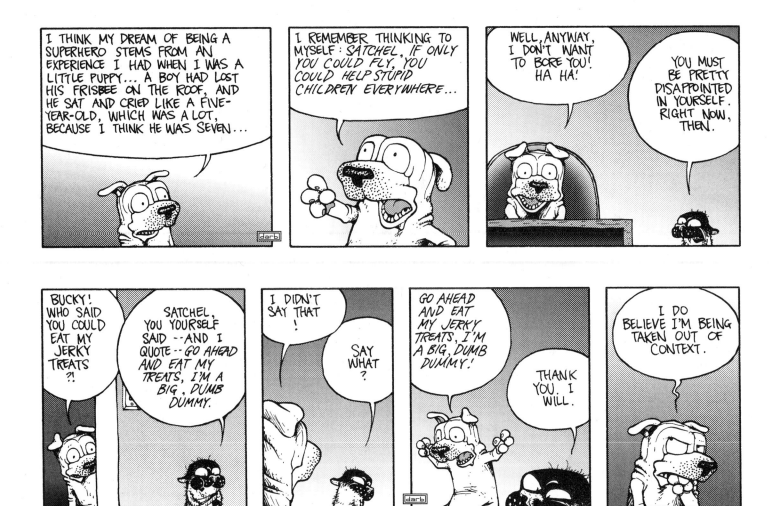

I THINK MY DREAM OF BEING A SUPERHERO STEMS FROM AN EXPERIENCE I HAD WHEN I WAS A LITTLE PUPPY... A BOY HAD LOST HIS FRISBEE ON THE ROOF, AND HE SAT AND CRIED LIKE A FIVE-YEAR-OLD, WHICH WAS A LOT, BECAUSE I THINK HE WAS SEVEN...

I REMEMBER THINKING TO MYSELF: SATCHEL, IF ONLY YOU COULD FLY, YOU COULD HELP STUPID CHILDREN EVERYWHERE...

WELL, ANYWAY, I DON'T WANT TO BORE YOU! HA HA!

YOU MUST BE PRETTY DISAPPOINTED IN YOURSELF. RIGHT NOW, THEN.

BUCKY! WHO SAID YOU COULD EAT MY JERKY TREATS?!

SATCHEL, YOU YOURSELF SAID -- AND I QUOTE -- GO AHEAD AND EAT MY TREATS, I'M A BIG, DUMB DUMMY.

I DIDN'T SAY THAT!

SAY WHAT?

GO AHEAD AND EAT MY JERKY TREATS, I'M A BIG, DUMB DUMMY!

THANK YOU. I WILL.

I DO BELIEVE I'M BEING TAKEN OUT OF CONTEXT.

HAVE YOU SEEN MY LAST BAG OF JERKY TREATS? I JUST SAW BUCKY AND HE DIDN'T HAVE IT.

FUNNY YOU SHOULD ASK. I JUST FOUND AN EMPTY JERKY BAG IN BUCKY'S DRESSER.

ARE YOU SAYING...

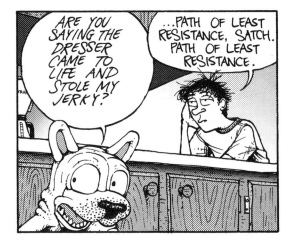

ARE YOU SAYING THE DRESSER CAME TO LIFE AND STOLE MY JERKY?

...PATH OF LEAST RESISTANCE, SATCH. PATH OF LEAST RESISTANCE.

58

59

63

MOM SAID SHE WAS FEDEXING YOU A BUNCH OF FRUIT AND COOKIES AND STUFF.

OH. I TOLD HER NOT TO OVERNIGHT ME A BUNCH OF FOOD!

YEAH, THAT'S WHERE SHE GOT THE IDEA.

FEDEXED FRESH COOKIES. I WONDER IF THEY'LL STILL BE WARM...THAT WOULD BE SURREAL.

NO, THE RAMONES USED IN AN AT&T COMMERCIAL - NOW THAT'S SURREAL.

SURREAL? SURREAL IS HOW EVEN THE VOMIT BUCKETS ON *FEAR FACTOR* HAVE THE SHOW'S LOGO ON THEM.

WHERE'S ROGER WILCO? I WANT DINNER.

MY BROTHER LEFT. SATCHEL'S COOKING TONIGHT.

WHAT THE...? ARE YOU **MAD**? HAS THAT BACK INJURY SPREAD TO YOUR HEAD?

DINNER'S READY!

I HOPE EVERYBODY LIKES RAVIOLI! IT'S MY MOTHER'S RECIPE.

WHICH PART? THE **CHEF**, OR THE **BOYAR-DEE**?

I TOLD YOU SO

a public service announcement

HEADSETS ARE A GREAT WAY TO PREVENT HARMFUL RADIATION FROM MESSING UP YOUR HEAD.

...JUST DON'T GO AND PUT THE CELL PHONE IN YOUR **LAP**, IDIOT. WHOLE OTHER PROBLEM THERE.

WILCO STILL LOOPY ON PAIN KILLERS?

WELL, YEAH, I GUESS.

HEY, ROBBO. QUICK WORD ASSOCIATION GAME...

MOST UNDERAPPRECIATED COMEDIAN?

JAKE JOHANNSEN.

MOST UNDERAPPRECIATED ARTIST?

WALLY TRIPP.

MOST EMERGENCY CASH IS IN THE..?

OATMEAL CANISTER.

WELL, NOW, THAT'S JUST WRONG.

BUCKY IS LOOKIN' BIGGER THESE DAYS, ISN'T HE?

WELL, WHAT DO YOU EXPECT?

WHAT DO YOU MEAN "WHAT DO I EXPECT"?

AND JUST BY THE WAY, I'M NOT SURE HOW MUCH LONGER I CAN KEEP IT UP...

WHAT ARE YOU TALKING ABOUT?

HOW YOU TOLD BUCKY TO EAT HALF OF MY FOOD AT EVERY MEAL.

I DIDN'T TELL HIM THAT.

"TELL," WRITE A "MEMO," WHATEVER... IT DIDN'T LOOK LIKE YOUR WRITING, BUT WHAT WITH ALL THE MEDICATION YOU'RE ON...

BUCKY!

ARE YOU TELLIN' ME THAT BUCKY'S BEEN EATING 50% OF YOUR FOOD FOR 3 WEEKS?

WELL...UH... I'M NOT REAL GOOD AT MATH, BUT HE'S BEEN EATING HALF OF IT, ANYWAY.

I DIDN'T TELL HIM HE COULD EAT ANY OF YOUR FOOD, SATCHEL.

THEN...HE'S JUST BEEN TAKING HALF OF MY FOOD AND LETTING ME STAY HUNGRY?

BUT WHY? WHY WOULD HE DO SUCH A THING?

...ARE YOU NEW HERE?

PROTECT YOUR HOME!

STUDIES SHOW THAT HOMES WITH DOGS ARE, LIKE, A MILLION TIMES LESS LIKELY TO BE BROKEN INTO.* HERE AT YE OLDE FUZZY COMIC AND HEAVY INDUSTRIES, WE CARE! TO PROTECT *YOUR* HOME, SIMPLY CUT OUT THESE ANTI-BURGLAR IMAGES AND PLACE THEM IN AN ENTRY WINDOW!**

* number provided for alarming effect only
** results not guaranteed

BEWARE OF DOG!

- dog more vicious than it appears.
- Y.O.F.C.H.I., Inc. not liable for any losses. darb

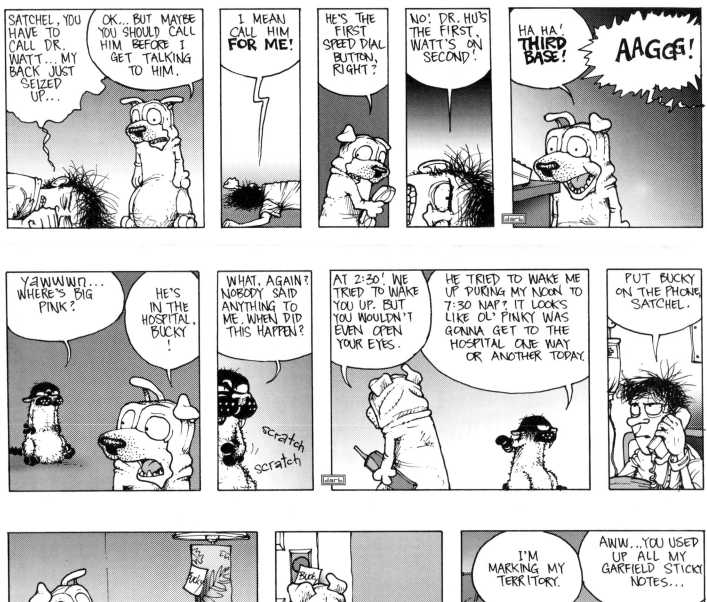

random cat facts

- SIR ISAAC NEWTON IS CREDITED WITH INVENTING THE CAT FLAP. WHO KNEW.

- CATS CAN HEAR ULTRASONIC FREQUENCIES, BUT ARE LOUSY AT DESCRIBING THEM.

- CAT URINE GLOWS UNDER A BLACK LIGHT, WHICH RAISES THE QUESTION "WHAT WEIRDO FIGURED THAT OUT?"

- CATS, CAMELS, AND GIRAFFES ARE THE ONLY ANIMALS WHO WALK BY MOVING BOTH RIGHT LEGS TOGETHER AND BOTH LEFT LEGS TOGETHER. FREAKS.

WORLD CAT FACTS

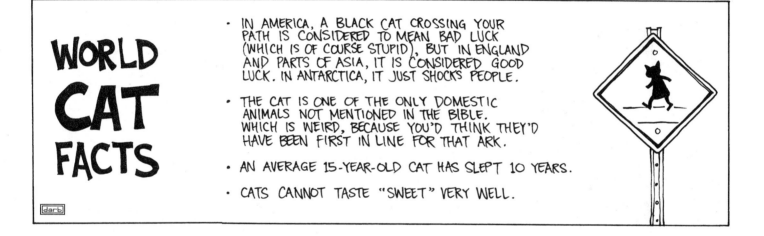

- IN AMERICA, A BLACK CAT CROSSING YOUR PATH IS CONSIDERED TO MEAN BAD LUCK (WHICH IS OF COURSE STUPID), BUT IN ENGLAND AND PARTS OF ASIA, IT IS CONSIDERED GOOD LUCK. IN ANTARCTICA, IT JUST SHOCKS PEOPLE.

- THE CAT IS ONE OF THE ONLY DOMESTIC ANIMALS NOT MENTIONED IN THE BIBLE. WHICH IS WEIRD, BECAUSE YOU'D THINK THEY'D HAVE BEEN FIRST IN LINE FOR THAT ARK.

- AN AVERAGE 15-YEAR-OLD CAT HAS SLEPT 10 YEARS.

- CATS CANNOT TASTE "SWEET" VERY WELL.

THEM Kitty bodies

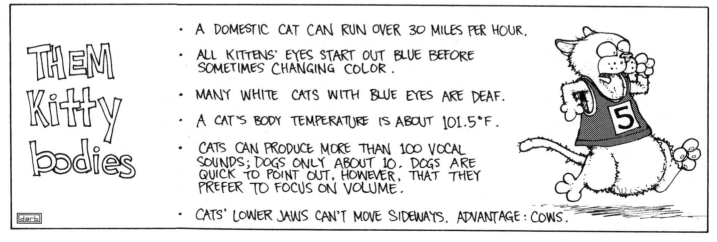

- A DOMESTIC CAT CAN RUN OVER 30 MILES PER HOUR.

- ALL KITTENS' EYES START OUT BLUE BEFORE SOMETIMES CHANGING COLOR.

- MANY WHITE CATS WITH BLUE EYES ARE DEAF.

- A CAT'S BODY TEMPERATURE IS ABOUT 101.5°F.

- CATS CAN PRODUCE MORE THAN 100 VOCAL SOUNDS; DOGS ONLY ABOUT 10. DOGS ARE QUICK TO POINT OUT, HOWEVER, THAT THEY PREFER TO FOCUS ON VOLUME.

- CATS' LOWER JAWS CAN'T MOVE SIDEWAYS. ADVANTAGE: COWS.

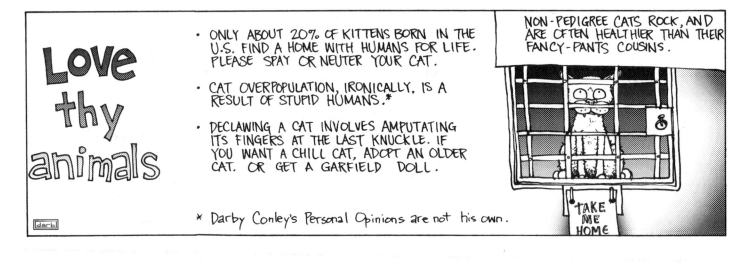

Love thy animals

- ONLY ABOUT 20% OF KITTENS BORN IN THE U.S. FIND A HOME WITH HUMANS FOR LIFE. PLEASE SPAY OR NEUTER YOUR CAT.

- CAT OVERPOPULATION, IRONICALLY, IS A RESULT OF STUPID HUMANS.*

- DECLAWING A CAT INVOLVES AMPUTATING ITS FINGERS AT THE LAST KNUCKLE. IF YOU WANT A CHILL CAT, ADOPT AN OLDER CAT. OR GET A GARFIELD DOLL.

* Darby Conley's Personal Opinions are not his own.

NON-PEDIGREE CATS ROCK, AND ARE OFTEN HEALTHIER THAN THEIR FANCY-PANTS COUSINS.

TAKE ME HOME

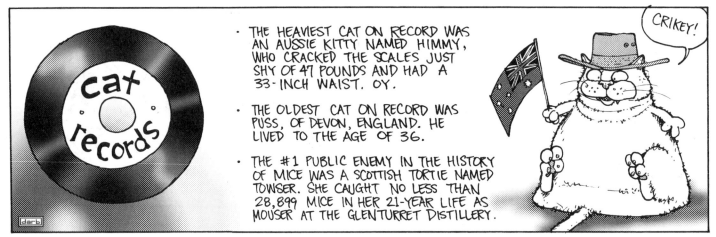

cat records

- THE HEAVIEST CAT ON RECORD WAS AN AUSSIE KITTY NAMED HIMMY, WHO CRACKED THE SCALES JUST SHY OF 47 POUNDS AND HAD A 33-INCH WAIST. OY.

- THE OLDEST CAT ON RECORD WAS PUSS, OF DEVON, ENGLAND. HE LIVED TO THE AGE OF 36.

- THE #1 PUBLIC ENEMY IN THE HISTORY OF MICE WAS A SCOTTISH TORTIE NAMED TOWSER. SHE CAUGHT NO LESS THAN 28,899 MICE IN HER 21-YEAR LIFE AS MOUSER AT THE GLENTURRET DISTILLERY.

CRIKEY!

CATS in ANCIENT EGYPT

- THE EGYPTIAN WORD FOR "CAT" IS "MAU", WHICH MEANS "SEER." ANCIENT EGYPTIANS BELIEVED CATS POSSESSED MYSTICAL POWER AND REVERED THEM. WHEN A CAT DIED, ITS HUMAN FAMILY WOULD SHAVE THEIR EYEBROWS IN A SIGN OF MOURNING.

- TODAY, WE KNOW THAT CATS ARE JUST STUCK-UP FREELOADERS.

BOBBIE, the WONDER DOG of OREGON

Bobbie

FROM AUGUST, 1923, TO FEBRUARY, 1924, A SCOTCH COLLIE-ENGLISH SHEPHERD MIX NAMED BOBBIE MADE PERHAPS THE MOST INCREDIBLE DOCUMENTED JOURNEY TO RETURN HOME. WHILE VISITING INDIANA, BOBBIE WAS CHASED AWAY FROM HIS OWNERS BY A PACK OF LOCAL DOGS. AFTER 3 WEEKS OF SEARCHING, HIS FAMILY WAS FORCED TO RETURN TO OREGON WITHOUT HIM, BROKEN-HEARTED. EXACTLY 6 MONTHS LATER, BOBBIE WALKED BACK INTO HIS HOMETOWN OF SILVERTON, OREGON, TIRED AND EMACIATED. HE HAD TRAVELED SOMEWHERE AROUND 3,000 MILES ON FOOT - THROUGH ICY RIVERS, SNOW STORMS AND OVER HUGE MOUNTAIN RANGES. AS HIS STORY BECAME KNOWN, HIS OWNERS RECEIVED MANY LETTERS FROM PEOPLE WHO HAD SEEN AND/OR HELPED BOBBIE ALONG HIS CROSS COUNTRY JOURNEY.

L'Histoire du CHIEN

- DOGS WERE PERHAPS THE FIRST DOMESTICATED ANIMAL. THEY HAVE LIVED AND WORKED WITH HUMANS FOR AT LEAST 12,000 YEARS.

- SALUKI-LIKE DOGS ARE REPRESENTED IN SUMERIAN ARTWORK AS OLD AS 7000 B.C.E.

- GEORGE WASHINGTON IS CONSIDERED THE FATHER OF THE AMERICAN FOXHOUND.

- THE COMICAL POODLE CUT WAS ORIGINALLY INTENDED TO AID THE DOG'S SWIMMING ABILITIES. THE POMS WERE LEFT TO KEEP THEIR JOINTS WARM.

- THE ONLY DOG TO APPEAR IN ONE OF SHAKESPEARE'S PLAYS WAS CRAB IN "THE TWO GENTLEMEN OF VERONA."

random DOG facts

ULULAT.

- THE CANARY ISLANDS WERE NOT NAMED AFTER BIRDS. THEY WERE NAMED AFTER THE LARGE DOGS THAT LIVED THERE IN ANCIENT TIMES: CANARIAE INSULAE = ISLAND OF DOGS

- THE EXPRESSION "THREE DOG NIGHT" IS AN ESKIMO EXPRESSION MEANING THAT IT'S SO COLD OUT THAT YOU HAVE TO HUDDLE WITH THREE DOGS TO STAY WARM.

- THE ROMANS BELIEVED THAT SIRIUS - THE DOG STAR - ADDED TO THE HEAT OF THE SUN GREATLY FROM JULY 3rd TO AUGUST 11th, CREATING THE DIES CANICULARES - THE DOG DAYS OF SUMMER.

Dogs in War.

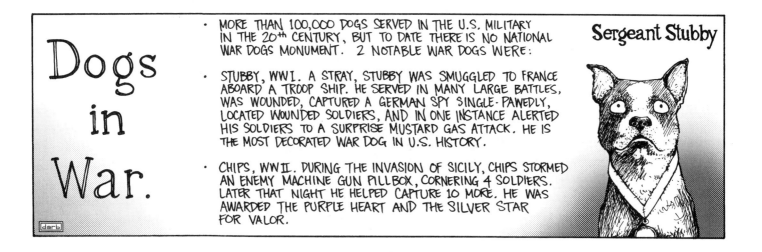

Sergeant Stubby

- MORE THAN 100,000 DOGS SERVED IN THE U.S. MILITARY IN THE 20th CENTURY, BUT TO DATE THERE IS NO NATIONAL WAR DOGS MONUMENT. 2 NOTABLE WAR DOGS WERE:

- STUBBY, WWI. A STRAY, STUBBY WAS SMUGGLED TO FRANCE ABOARD A TROOP SHIP. HE SERVED IN MANY LARGE BATTLES, WAS WOUNDED, CAPTURED A GERMAN SPY SINGLE-PAWEDLY, LOCATED WOUNDED SOLDIERS, AND IN ONE INSTANCE ALERTED HIS SOLDIERS TO A SURPRISE MUSTARD GAS ATTACK. HE IS THE MOST DECORATED WAR DOG IN U.S. HISTORY.

- CHIPS, WWII. DURING THE INVASION OF SICILY, CHIPS STORMED AN ENEMY MACHINE GUN PILLBOX, CORNERING 4 SOLDIERS. LATER THAT NIGHT HE HELPED CAPTURE 10 MORE. HE WAS AWARDED THE PURPLE HEART AND THE SILVER STAR FOR VALOR.

dog records

- THE HEAVIEST DOG ON RECORD WAS AN OLD ENGLISH MASTIFF NAMED ZORBA, WHO WEIGHED 343 POUNDS AND MEASURING 8 FEET, 3 INCHES FROM HEAD TO TAIL, IS ALSO THE LONGEST DOG ON RECORD AS WELL.

- THE SMALLEST DOG EVER RECORDED WAS A YORKIE FROM BLACKBURN, ENGLAND. AT 2 YEARS OLD, HE WAS ONLY 2.5 INCHES HIGH AND 3.75 INCHES LONG. HE TIPPED THE SCALES AT JUST 4 OUNCES.

- THE OLDEST DOG RELIABLY RECORDED WAS BLUEY, AN AUSTRALIAN CATTLE DOG WHO LIVED FOR 29 YEARS AND 5 MONTHS – ALMOST 20 OF THOSE YEARS SPENT AT *WORK.*

Doggie Physiology

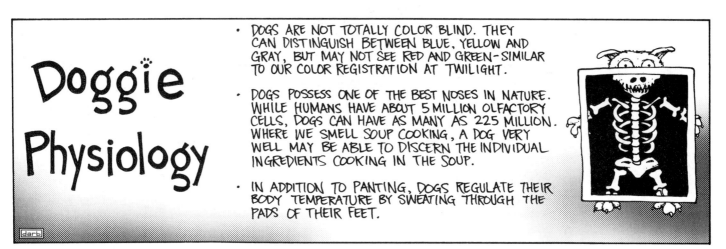

- DOGS ARE NOT TOTALLY COLOR BLIND. THEY CAN DISTINGUISH BETWEEN BLUE, YELLOW AND GRAY, BUT MAY NOT SEE RED AND GREEN – SIMILAR TO OUR COLOR REGISTRATION AT TWILIGHT.

- DOGS POSSESS ONE OF THE BEST NOSES IN NATURE. WHILE HUMANS HAVE ABOUT 5 MILLION OLFACTORY CELLS, DOGS CAN HAVE AS MANY AS 225 MILLION. WHERE WE SMELL SOUP COOKING, A DOG VERY WELL MAY BE ABLE TO DISCERN THE INDIVIDUAL INGREDIENTS COOKING IN THE SOUP.

- IN ADDITION TO PANTING, DOGS REGULATE THEIR BODY TEMPERATURE BY SWEATING THROUGH THE PADS OF THEIR FEET.

WHY DOES THIS GUY ON TV KEEP SAYING "CAN YOU HEAR ME NOW?"

THIS IS A CELL PHONE AD. THAT'S THEIR SLOGAN.

WHY? ARE THEIR PHONES SO BAD NO ONE CAN EVER HEAR YOU?

NO, THEY'RE FINE. THAT'S THE ONE I HAVE.

WELL, THAT SLOGAN MAKES THEM SOUND PROBLEMATIC.

IT OUGHT TO BE "STOP YELLING INTO THE PHONE!" OR "DO YOU HAVE A COLD? I DETECT A SLIGHT DEVIATION FROM THE WAY YOU USUALLY SOUND."

HOW 'BOUT JUST "LOUD AND CLEAR"?

OOO, THAT'S NOT BAD... I COULD SELL THAT TO THEM AND MAKE A FORTUNE.

I'LL CALL THEM AND PASS THAT ALONG.

PSSH. GOOD LUCK GETTING THROUGH. I'LL CALL THEM MYSELF. WHERE ARE THE STAMPS?

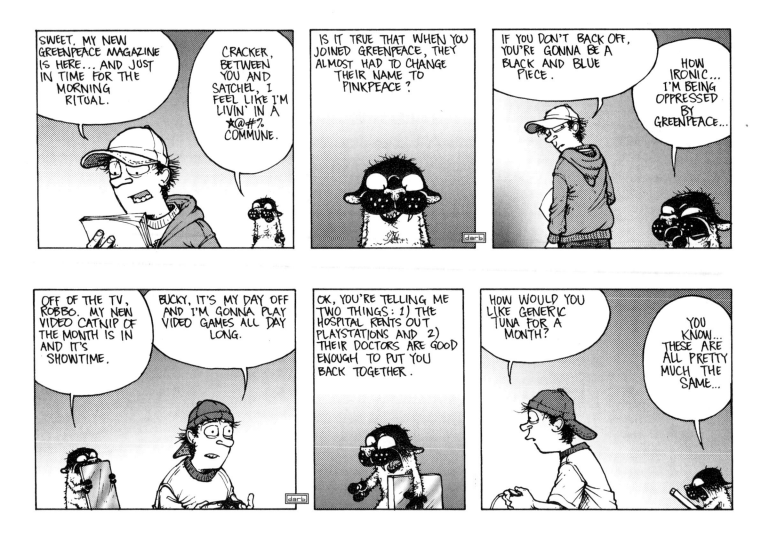

82

...SO BUCKY DOESN'T WANT TO GO WITH US ON VACATION AND HE WAS WONDERING IF HE COULD STAY WITH YOU...MM-HM...OK, THANKS DAD.

NO GO. HE SAYS HE'S HAVING HIS HAIR DONE THAT WEEK.

WELL, OK, IT... ...WAIT... YOUR DAD IS BALD...

$2+2=...$

MIGHT HE STILL BE MAD ABOUT THE PUDDING INCIDENT?

ONE MIGHT REASONABLY INFER.

ROB WILCO, AFTER CAREFUL CONSIDERATION OF YOUR PROPOSED VACATION, I'M AFRAID THAT I, SATCHEL POOCH, HAVE TO REQUEST THAT WE NOT GO.

GEE, SATCH, I THOUGHT YOU WERE EXCITED TO GO TO MAINE...NO ONE PUT YOU UP TO THIS, DID THEY?

MR. WILCO, I COME TO YOU ON MY OWN FREE ...UM...FREE...

WILL.

YOU DO REALIZE THAT MAINE IS ONE OF THE SEAFOOD CAPITALS OF THE WORLD, RIGHT "SATCHEL"?

MR. WILCO, I MUST INSIST—

ABORT! ABORT!

DO YOU HAVE AN, UM, CHAMBER REAMER I CAN BORROW?

A WHAT? WHAT FOR?

BUCKY'S TAKING HIS GUN REPAIR CLASS HOMEWORK WITH HIM ON VACATION.

OH, OK. WELL, I DON'T.....

HOLD ON, WHAT NOW?

WE DON'T HAVE TO GO THROUGH CUSTOMS TO GET TO MAINE, DO WE?

Panel 1: SO YOU GAVE BUCKY THIS SQUIRT GUN FOR A FAKE GUN REPAIR CLASS?

I RESENT THAT. THE MEGA-WETTER IS A DELICATE MACHINE.

Panel 2: WAIT A SEC... YOU'RE THE GUY WHO CHUCKS ON EVERYBODY'S DOORSTEP IN THE MIDDLE OF THE NIGHT... YOU'RE THE CHUCKER.

I PREFER CHARLES.

Panel 3: ...AND I COULD SET YOU UP WITH A GOOD HAIRDRESSING WORKSHOP IF YOU'D—

SCRAM, CHUCKER.

Panel 4: I'M TRYING TO PACK WARM CLOTHES FOR MAINE—DO YOU LIKE THIS SHIRT?

IF YOU WEAR THAT SHIRT IN PUBLIC— AND I KID YOU NOT— YOU WILL BE SHAMED LIKE A CHILD ACTOR IN A BED-WETTING COMMERCIAL.

Panel 5: I DON'T THINK IT'S ANY SILLIER THAN YOUR HAT...

SATCHEL, WHEN I WANT YOUR OPINION, I'LL GIVE IT TO YOU.

Panel 6: WELL, HOW ABOUT THIS SHIRT I GOT FROM FUNGO?

I....OH MY HEAD... OH, MY BEAUTIFUL HEAD...

Panel 7: OOOO, HA! HA! BOOM! LOOK AT ALL THE PRETTY SPARKS!!

DON'T CLAP AT THAT!

CLAP CLAP

Panel 8: WASN'T THAT A FIREWORK? OR PERFORMANCE ART?

NAW, MAN, THAT WAS SOME IDIOT THROWING A CIGARETTE OUT OF HIS CAR.

GOOD ONE, SATCH.

Panel 9: MY STRENGTH IS THAT I CAN LAUGH AT MYSELF, BUCKY.

YOUR WEAKNESS IS THAT YOU DON'T HAVE A CHOICE.

ENOUGH!

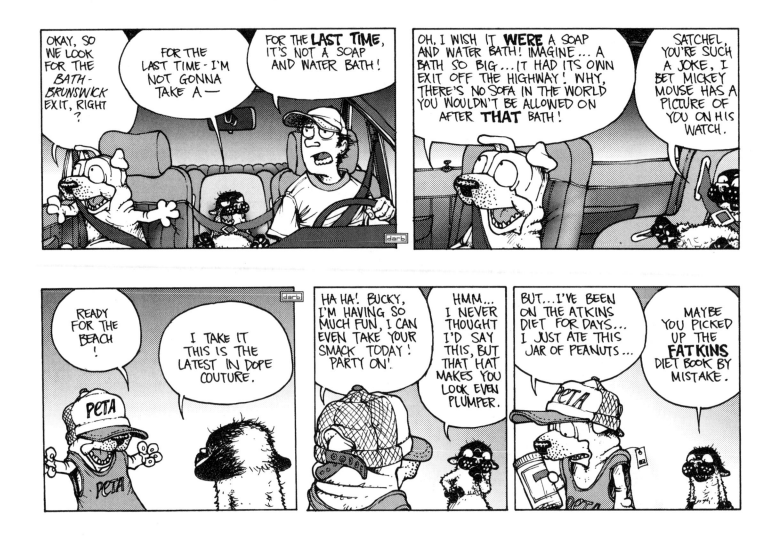

91

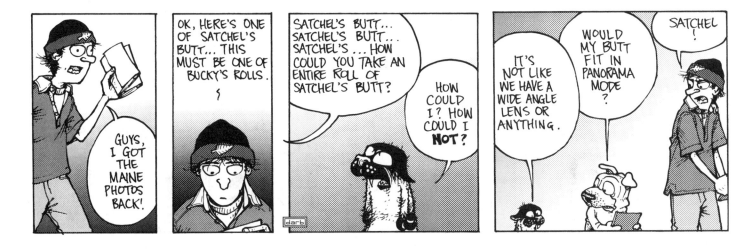

GUYS, I GOT THE MAINE PHOTOS BACK!

OK, HERE'S ONE OF SATCHEL'S BUTT... THIS MUST BE ONE OF BUCKY'S ROLLS.

SATCHEL'S BUTT... SATCHEL'S BUTT... SATCHEL'S ... HOW COULD YOU TAKE AN ENTIRE ROLL OF SATCHEL'S BUTT?

HOW COULD I? HOW COULD I NOT?

IT'S NOT LIKE WE HAVE A WIDE ANGLE LENS OR ANYTHING.

WOULD MY BUTT FIT IN PANORAMA MODE?

SATCHEL!

HERE ARE THE PICTURES FROM THE MARINE CENTER.

TOUCH A LIVE LOBSTER $1.00

I LOVED THAT LOBSTER!

BEST LOBSTER EVER.

I HEAR YOU SAY "MMMM," I TAKE IT YOU LIKE MY CHILI?

TECHNICALLY, I WENT HMMMM...

..AND I'M NOT GONNA SAY IT'S BAD...

BUT THAT'S BECAUSE I HAVE TO GO THROW UP...

95

96

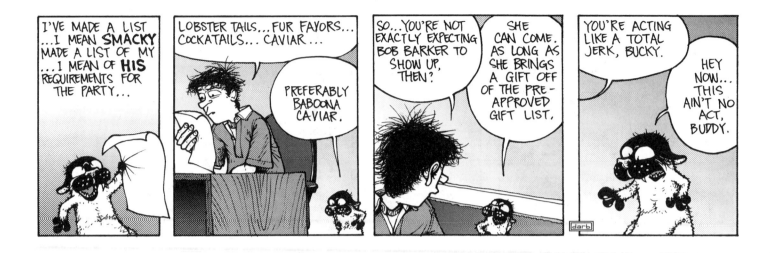

100

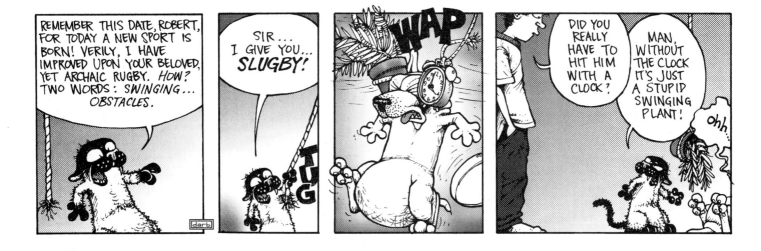

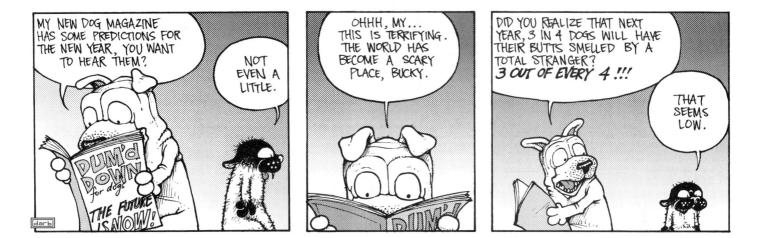

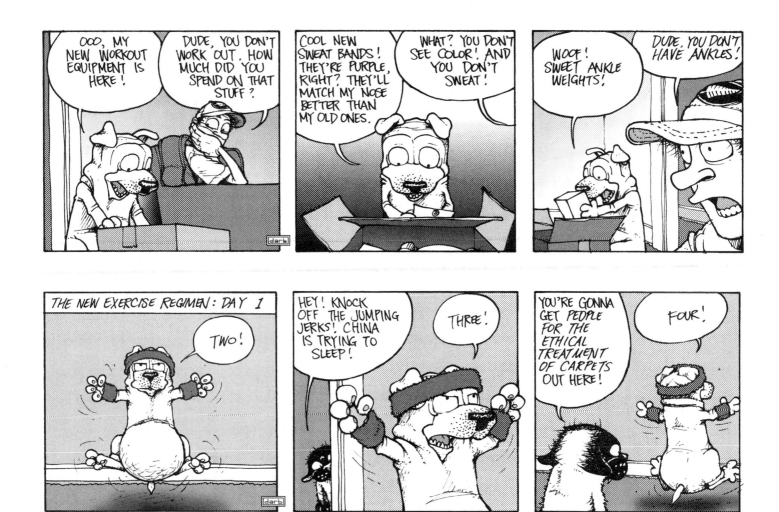

127